KU-132-910

The Town & County Book of
Scotland

The Town & County Book of
Scotland

PHOTOGRAPHS BY FREDERICK BLOEMENDAL

TEXT BY JOHN MACKAY

LONDON

A Member of the Ian Allan Group

Bibliography

An Edinburgh Alphabet, J. F. Birrell (James Thin)

Scottish Diaries and Memories 1550-1746, J. G. Fyfe (Mackay, Stirling)

We Scots, John Mackay (Chambers)

A History of Scotland for Today, Gould & Thompson (John Murray)

Scotland's Magazine, passim

First published 1985

ISBN 0 86364 029 X

All rights reserved. No part of this book may be
reproduced or transmitted in any form or by any
means, electronic or mechanical, including photo-
copying, recording or by any information storage
and retrieval system, without permission from the
Publisher in writing.

Photographs © F. A. H. Bloemendal 1984

© Ian Allan Ltd 1985

Published by Town & County Books , Shepperton, Surrey;
and printed in Italy by
Graphische Betriebe Athesia, Bolzano

INTRODUCTION

This introduction is aimed first of all at the visitor.

The native, whether he or she is in this country or exiled somewhere across the Border, will understand that before commenting on people and places of interest to all, we must explain to the visitor or tourist where so many of their contemporaries of recent times went wrong when they came to Scotland. And we can do it in one sentence, as follows.

They sped across the Border heading for Edinburgh then shot up into the Highlands and the far northwest.

This book of camera studies shows what they missed, last time.

Let's go on a tour — a clockwise route, beginning at the most dramatic threshold into Scotland — on the boundary line at Carter Bar on the A68, where the broad moorland below rises north to the first of Scotland's hills. The Borders are, roughly, that area with its base along the line of the Cheviot hills and its northern outpost, the Lammermuir range.

To appreciate the Borders fully it is necessary to give some space to the Border reiver or mosstrooper, for he it was, who, along with his womenfolk like Mary Scott the 'Flower of Yarrow' — inspired many of the Border ballads and who built up the peel towers above the rivers and thus gave added character to many a Border scene.

These steel-bonneted horsemen had their heyday at the end of the 16th century but persisted into the 17th when Cromwell complained that they were — 'basely and inhumanly murdering my men'; and even in the 18th century an antiquarian working at Hadrian's Wall in Northumbria, complained that his studies were disturbed by 'the rascal mosstroopers thereabouts'.

The reiver chiefs, like their Highland counterparts were remote enough from royal authority to lay down their own laws and pronounce judgement on their offending adherents. Wardens were, in fact, appointed by the Crown to police the Borders, but since these Wardens of the Marches were often reiver chiefs themselves, this was not always a success. Even so, the Warden met his English opposite number each year to decide solemnly whose cattle had been stolen by whom (or ladies abducted for that matter?); who deserved compensation, and who deserved hanging — if he could be caught. Carter Bar itself was one of the meeting places.

From Carter Bar, the way is open to the Border towns including Langholm, Hawick, Selkirk, Galashiels, Innerleithen, Melrose, Lauder, Kelso, Coldstream and Duns. All these have their summer festivals or riding of the marches when some incident in their past history is commemorated; for example, the ceremony of the 'Casting of the Colours' at Selkirk is a lament for the lone standard-bearer who returned from the defeat at Flodden.

The 'marches' were the boundaries of the family lands or parishes zealously and regularly patrolled in the old days when land grabbers as well as cattle thieves were about. Today, this patrol is maintained as a tradition once a year when even a small burgh like Lauder can muster over 200 horses for the celebrations.

Time now to be on our way by Jedburgh and on to Kelso where incidentally the nearby village of Ednam was the birthplace of James Thomson who wrote the words of *Rule Britannia* and H. F. Lyte who wrote *Abide With Me*.

From Kelso, west to Smailholm Tower the most impressively sited of all the Border keeps or peel towers, and still charged with the atmosphere of those reiver days, with cattle grazing on the surrounding moorland.

The boy Walter Scott holidayed at Sandyknowe farm near the Tower and his youthful imagination was fired on his first hearing of the tales of the Borderland.

A new attraction at the recently refurbished Tower is the permanent exhibition of characters from Sir Walter Scott's novels and poems. These figurines dressed in the fabrics proper to their time are much more than dolls — more like miniature creations of the characters, come to life. All are the work of Anne Carrick whose sculptor father fashioned the statue of Sir William Wallace at the entrance to Edinburgh Castle.

From Smailholm to Scott's favourite view and on to the Abbeys of Dryburgh and Melrose, then to the bustling tweed town of Galashiels whose war memorial features an equestrian statue of the Border Reiver. The steel bonneted warrior symbolically represents the Border soldier from ancient times to the present day. Sculptor Clapperton created this work, and his is the statue of the Bruce beside the one of Wallace in Edinburgh.

Before heading for Peebles, a southwest divergence to near Selkirk to mention 'Muckle Mou'd Meg' (Big Mouthed Meg). Willie Scott of Oakwood, captured on a raid on Murray property was given a choice: hang, or marry Murray's daughter. Willie took one look at Meg of the large mouth and chose to hang. But on the morning of the execution he changed his mind. The marriage was a success. He had 'grown accustomed to her face'? Oakwood Tower,

Willie's former home, is still intact by the roadside. This is near Bowhill, a seat of the Duke of Buccleuch — one of the many stately homes and castles open to visitors in the Borders; these include Traquair, the oldest inhabited house in Britain (with its own brew of beer) which is on our route as, returning from Peebles, we go south at Innerleithen, to Yarrow and St Mary's Loch. Then by the Devil's Beef Tub ('beef tub' — a place to hide cattle) to join the A74 below Moffat for Thomas Carlyle's birthplace at Ecclefechan.

West now, for Dumfries and Galloway.

Dumfries has lasting associations with Robert Burns. The house he lived in is open to visitors; and the Globe Inn a favoured hostelry of the poet's, continues to dispense cheer. Included with other attractions, the museum built round a former windmill where the grounds disclose statuary and busts in unexpected places.

Before leaving Dumfries for the west, the coast road south on the east bank of the River Nith leads to the lovely moated ruin of Caerlaverock adjoining a national nature reserve.

On the other side of the Nith after leaving Sweetheart Abbey, tourists from the USA may be interested in visiting the cottage at Kirkbean where that sometime-pirate Paul Jones was born — the man who founded the American Navy.

What Cornwall is to England, so Galloway is to Scotland: sometimes withdrawn, sometimes mysterious, where the dark wide sands of Solway flood with a racing tide turning the whole Firth to gold in a morning light. And inland, beyond the patterned fields, the secret places under the hills lying grape-blue in shadow. A land too in times remote that fostered the dawn of Christianity — the land of St Ninian. Between Portpatrick and the Mull of Galloway, evidence of these early days in what must be the strangest of all 'showcases': sealed in by heavy plate glass in the porch of the deserted church of Kirkmadrine, a group of strangely carved Christian grave stones thought to be over 1,500 years old. In more holiday vein on the same narrow strip above the Mull, the Logan Botanic Garden; and at the Logan Fish Pond one can feed the residents by hand — not goldfish, but *cod*.

Galloway has for long been artists' country with its wide variety of scenic effects — and perhaps by the pictorial oddities that occur, conjured up by the irregular coastline and the twisting rivers to produce for example the curious sight at Palnackie of a small bright funnel presumably attached to a cargo boat, apparently sailing along the far side of a field.

From Galloway, north into the true Burns Country — the Ayrshire pastoral, producing as an offshoot of this richly agricultural land and well sprung coastal turf, championship golf courses at Turnberry and Troon.

In Ayrshire it is the houses and farms associated with the poet, much more than the sometimes overdressed monuments around, that are his better memorials — his best memorial of course, his poetry. In the Burns Centre at Alloway, the theatre presents a multiscreen story of his life and times.

Burns's poetic range is wider than often thought. Here is a line or two from a poem on whether the moon is created anew each time it appears or whether there is more than one. When he imagines shepherds discussing this, is he anticipating the astronaut of today when, deciding to settle the argument he sends them up . . .

> '. . . in things they ca' balloons,
>   to tak a flight;
> An' stay ae month amang the moons
>   An' see them right.'

If we keep to the route linked by the photographer's chosen subject matter, this means that on leaving Largs we can contrive to arrive on the western suburbs of Glasgow and so aim for Pollok Country Park before entering the city. The park is worth aiming for, since it now contains the Burrell Art Collection — the newest of Glasgow's art galleries and unique in its sylvan setting.

Glasgow is an ideal stepping off place for the Highlands and for Stirling, the gateway to that region. To pass through Stirling on the main road without turning uphill left in the town would be a serious mistake, for up there apart from the historic buildings in, and outwith the castle, there's a new Landmark Centre adding to the displays already a feature of the castle approaches, visually causing the old Royal Burgh to come alive again for the visitor.

Now by Aberfoyle to Loch Arklet and here, as in the days of Rob Roy whose headquarters were in these parts, there are not many roads for motor cars. One is in a Highland fastness here and thoughts turn to the Highlandman who lived in these wilds when the tartan was not just the decorative part of a man's outfit hung from the waist but the *filleadh mòr* (great kilt) a complete garment and a camouflage that merged with the heather and bracken slopes — a garment that matched with the great sword, popularly called today, the 'claymore'.

As we trace our route back to Aberfoyle then by Loch Katrine, Callander, Lochearnhead, Crianlarich, Tyndrum and arrive in Glencoe, we are in the Glen that, in the days of the great sword, saw 'the Massacre'.

The government of that time ordered the clan chiefs to take an oath of allegiance to William III by the last day of December 1691; but guessing that such allegiance would not be forthcoming, prepared plans for another method of subduing the Highlands. The expeditionary force sent north were instructed — 'by fire and sword and all manner of hostility to burn their houses, seize and burn their cattle, plenishing or clothes, and cut down the men'.

The MacDonalds of Glencoe were chosen as a lesson to the other clans, and the massacre began 'by fire and sword' at five o'clock on the morning of 12 February 1692. The surprise assault was directed by Campbell of Glenlyon who, with his men, had been hospitably received a few days before by the MacDonalds.

And what of the Highlander when he came south and crossed the Border in 1745? Rumour was rife in Cumbria on his expected behaviour — and very much exaggerated; thus, as an officer of the Prince — David, Lord Elcho, billeted in Carlisle and by no means a savage, recorded in a diary of the time: 'Their (sic) was an old woman remained in a house that night where some officers were quarter'd. After they had sup'd, she said to them, Gentlemen, I suppose You have done with Your murdering today, I should be Glad to know when the *ravishing* begins.'

Returning to the main route at Crianlarich we then head northeast by Loch Tay to Pitlochry (a tourist centre in itself) and on to Glenshee where the chair lift for the skiers in winter, can operate in summer for those bent on climbing — the easy way.

So, to Braemar and 'Royal Deeside' where Highland gatherings reign supreme — their advent heralded by the heather as it comes into bloom — then on by the castles of Craigievar and Crathes, to Aberdeen.

Aberdeen is in the news these days with the oil boom, but there's a more lasting industry here — the fishing. The first steam drifter was built in Aberdeen in 1868 and trawling was centred in the city from 1882. By the year 1913, 200 trawlers were operating from the harbour. Aberdeen remains one of the leading fishing ports in Scotland but the industry has been fined down since the days of the 200 trawlers.

In contrast, a flying visit north to a miniature fishing port on the sea coast east of the Moray Firth, in the Grampian region — a region which has its share of the 'whisky trail' — a tour of the distilleries; and eastward on that coast before returning to Aberdeen, that extraordinary cliff formation known as the 'Bullers of Buchan'.

It is in the Buchan region that the local dialect is something to savour. Or *was* something to savour perhaps, since TV and radio have levelled out many native tongues. Although Aberdeen itself continues to charm with the speech peculiarly its own, and surely the country around still has something of the native way of expressing themselves?

Now on the way south by Stonehaven and Montrose where a short detour is recommended to Edzell Castle and in particular to its garden laid out in the 17th century formal manner; and where a chequered pattern of blue and white flowers against the red sandstone of carved walls contrives to show the heraldic colours of the Lindsay clan banner.

From Montrose to Arbroath, to Dundee and across the Tay keeping to the coast round to St Andrews. Nearby Leuchars has something for both the modern minded and the antiquarian inclined: a RAF fighter station and a church of ancient origin — a Norman rarity in stone.

Coming round the coast, Anstruther, next to Pittenweem, has the Scottish Fisheries Museum. And don't miss Crail or St Monance, this latter with a church interior of special interest in which a fine model of a sailing vessel suspends from the ceiling.

Across Fife now, inland to 'gracious old Falkland', to Loch Leven, Dunfermline, Culross and return to cross the Forth to South Queensferry, Linlithgow birthplace of Mary, Queen of Scots, and so to Edinburgh.

Of the Lothian Region, formerly West Lothian, Midlothian and East Lothian, East Lothian is the most colourful by virtue of its red soil and sandstone and its proximity to the widening blue of the Firth. This is why, as one skirts the coast on the way to the Border again, one should also look inland to such villages as Gifford and Stenton and to the town of Haddington and the National Trust's Preston Mill at East Linton — if one has time that is, before crossing the Border and ending the Scottish tour at 'The County and the Borough and Town of Berwick upon Tweed'.

John Mackay
Oxton, Lauder
Berwickshire, 1984

Jedburgh (Borders) Coming over the Border at Carter Bar and making their first stop in Scotland at Jedburgh, visitors who had been led to believe that Scottish towns are of a uniform grey are in for a surprise.

Jedburgh *was* like that once and due for a drastic demolishing of its old and sometimes derelict buildings. But in 1962, representatives from the Scottish Development Department and local councils, drew up plans to turn the High Street into a pedestrian precinct, divert the A68 trunk road clear of the town centre and restore the best of the old houses. In their report they showed — 'how a historic small burgh could be remodelled to meet the challenge of the motor age, while preserving its traditional quality and character'.

This has now been done.

Among many other restorations, 'Under Nag's Head Close' and 'Blackhills Close' where Prince Charlie spent a night in 1745, are notable, with the Market Place and Castlegate at the heart of the transformation. When I was last in Jedburgh, a party of schoolchildren from France newly come from nearby Mary, Queen of Scots' House, were window shopping in the Castlegate: an animated scene indeed, with such a background of colour.

Changed days from when Jedburgh, a frontier town, was being burned with enthusiasm at regular intervals from the south. After one of the many battles for Jedburgh, the Earl of Hertford wrote to Henry VIII — 'I assure your grace, I found the Scottes, the boldest men and the hotest that I ever saw in any nation'.

Kelso (Borders) Militant monks of Kelso Abbey once held out for two days against Hertford's force attacking with fire and cannon, bent on destroying the religious houses of the Scottish Borders. This photograph catches the contrast of today — the calm that shrouds these venerable stones of what was once the greatest abbey in all Scotland and, as seen by the Norman style of its architecture, one of the oldest.

The abbey is flanked on its north side by Kelso Square, with bull ring, and coaching inn; and enhanced by buildings of true Georgian grace, justifying the town's claim to be the fairest in the Borders. On the abbey's southern flank, the road crosses the River Tweed by John Rennie's bridge — the prototype for his Waterloo Bridge across the Thames. Looking upstream, Floors Castle, home of the Duke of Roxburgh, shows its imposing facade across broad parklands. At left, the River Teviot joins the Tweed.

Follow the Teviot to the miniature hill on which once stood Roxburgh Castle moated at one side by Tweed, on the other by Teviot and dominating a long vanished medieval town of the same name.

Today, the hill with castle ruins on top is mirrored in the still waters of Teviot. Looking upstream, the open landscape dissolves in light in days of high summer — as it did when once, standing by the bank, a small boy passed me with home made fishing tackle. 'Any luck', I asked. 'Twae wee ains' (two wee ones) was his reply — and he continued by the bank until, like the landscape itself, he seemed to dissolve in light.

10

Scott's View by Galashiels (Borders) Let us suppose we have come by Smailholm Tower and Dryburgh Abbey and have stopped, as Sir Walter Scott used often to do, to look at the view, triple crowned by the Eildon hills. In so doing, we have travelled the very heart of Scott's Borderland.

Here, the photographer has looked up the valley of the Tweed where Melrose and its abbey rise below Eildon's shadow and where the tweed town of Galashiels points the way to Scott's Abbotsford home. Lower right, the river flows darkly at a horseshoe bend on its way by Kelso to the sea.

Legend claims that Michael Scott, the Borders' medieval wizard split the Eildons in three, but the site of a Roman signal station on the nearest peak shown here and of a cavalry fort below, named by them 'Trimontium', spoils the wizard tale. Yet, a revengeful influence against his scoffers may still be abroad? This writer, after once penning an ironical paragraph on the magic claims made in Michael's name, suffered a bust camera while on Eildon's highest top; and later, working at the Scott view, a suddenly split sketching stool!

An extra here, for lovers of curiosities: retracing one's steps from the view and about half a mile at right, leave the road for a wood at the end of whose path, a 30ft high statue of Scotland's patriot Sir William Wallace appears through the foliage — an eccentric monument erected by an eccentric 11th Earl of Buchan. Despite its being praised by certain Scottish Nationalists, I cannot like this statue.

12   Sir Walter Scott didn't like it either.

Peebles (Borders) Continuing by Tweed to the Royal and Ancient Burgh of Peebles, pictured here from the path which goes upstream past Neidpath Castle (a typical Borders peel tower) to form an unspoiled natural riverside park.

The old parish church at the end of the High Street shows here its 'Crown Imperial' steeple. Arrayed on the steps in front of the church, the youth of the burgh in their summer's best, assemble each year for the crowning of the Beltane Queen. Long ago in Beltane (Baal) time fires were lit to pagan gods and feasting and sports were enjoyed in welcoming the return of the summer sun. The early Christian pioneers wisely retained such rites so popular with the masses, but steered the ceremonial to their own religious use. The crowning of today however, is simply a festival of youth — but allied to the week-long celebrations with the traditional Riding of the Marches.

Peebles takes pride in her distinguished sons. Mungo Park, explorer of the Niger had his surgery in the High Street. William Chambers, publisher of the far-famed dictionary gifted the art gallery, library and museum to the town. John Buchan, later Lord Tweedsmuir, taught in Sunday school here. A story tells how this author of *The Thirty-nine Steps* boasted a much bigger class than any of the other teachers. The reason was simple: after the Bible lesson, he finished with a little adventure story for his class — and always took care that it would stop at a 'to-be-continued-next-week' moment so that his pupils would be sure to return the following Sunday.

14

St Mary's Loch and Yarrow, Cappercleuch (Borders) This is ballad-haunted country. The photograph conveys its atmosphere of melancholy beauty.

The best known of all the Border ballads, *The Dowie Dens o' Yarrow*, did indeed haunt me in my formative years, for a series of engravings framed in ebony hung forbiddingly in the house of a relative. It told of the duel between a Scott of Tushielaw and a Scott of Thirlestane, this last mentioned saying as he set out for the duelling ground:

> *O fare ye weel, my ladye gaye*
> *O fare ye weel, my Sarah,*
> *From I mun gae though I ne're return*
> *From the dowie banks o' Yarrow.*

Nor did he. There follows a scene of lamentation and passion when the lady discovers his bloodied body. Strong stuff these ballads.

'Dowie' is a Scots word for 'sad', but all is not to be thought doleful here. James Hogg, 'the Ettrick shepherd' who gave the words of the *Dowie Dens* to Walter Scott, and who ranks high in Scotland as a self-educated poet of quality, enjoyed the company of other poets and learned professors at Tibby Shiel's inn by St Mary's Loch from where Yarrow flows to join Ettrick. Hogg, on the morning after one of their gatherings where drink, debate and discussion had run together into the small hours, would waken with the great thirst and hoarsely command the hostess — 'Tibbie! Bring in the *Loch*!'

Hogg was a real working shepherd too, and Yarrow is still sheep country; though gone are the days when shepherds would cross the long hill-miles to attend worship at lamp-lit Yarrow Kirk, with their dogs, cheek on paw, lying quiet under the pews.

Ecclefechan (Dumfries & Galloway) Thomas Carlyle's birthplace This dwelling is appropriate as the home of a master mason — self-made, and master of a growing family. Such a man was James Carlyle, a traditionalist in his respect for Scottish education of that time when it was normal to see the vilagers of Ecclefechan foregathering of an evening to debate theological matters.

There is, of course, another side to the picture: of the 20 'tippling houses' in the district to assuage the thirst of the wild drovers when they came to cattle markets at the end of the 18th century there; by which time James's son Thomas was five years old and ready for school.

Extraordinary to think that a little less than nine years later, Thomas was on his way to begin student days at university, walking the nearly hundred miles to Edinburgh in company of another lad — and occasional lifts when fatigued, were given by a man driving a cart loaded with potatoes. Thus, the once bare-footed boy who sang ballads to the village weavers while they worked, took the first steps towards his becoming 'The Sage of Chelsea' — an essayist and historian strongly influencing the thinking of his generation; and destined to return to that University of Edinburgh as Rector in 1865, beating Disraeli 657 votes to 310. His *History of the French Revolution* had to be rewritten from memory, for, on lending the manuscript before publication to his friend John Mill, Mill's maid, tidying her master's study, mistook the sheets for waste paper — and burned it!

Burial in Westminster Abbey was offered on his death in 1881, but Thomas Carlyle had instructed that he be buried without religious service beside his parents in Ecclefechan in Annandale.

The Auld Brig, Dumfries The gateway to Galloway, that choice region of the southwest, Dumfries has shown pride and concern for its bridge since early in the 15th century when penitents were made to give money towards its building by the burgesses and inhabitants. In 1609 the town council were worried by the 'force and violence of the water of Nith' against the bridge and upgraded the dues for its maintenance. For every horse or cow crossing, 16 pence; for every pack of goods, two shillings; for every barque coming up the Nith to the town, 13 shillings and four pence . . and so on. Today the bridge no longer takes traffic other than pedestrians, yet remains one of Dumfries's attractions for any visitor who appreciates the natural beauty of the stonework in these old river crossings.

In 1660, a barrel-maker built a house at the west, or in this view, extreme left of the bridge. Later it flourished as an inn where Robert Burns would call during his work as an exciseman. The Old Bridge House as it is now known, has become a small but fascinating museum of domestic life.

Council care continues to cosset the bridge, for in the 1960s, happening to be in Dumfries, I crossed to the west side to find out why divers were descending into the Nith. One arch of the bridge had partially collapsed and they were retrieving the fallen fabric stone by stone from the riverbed. The cost of bringing professional divers from the Clyde had been prohibitive — so, the local builder with the contract for the repairs, had two of his men trained to do the job themselves!

Sweetheart Abbey, New Abbey (Dumfries & Galloway) Crossing the Nith from Dumfries into the ancient kingdom of Galloway, one is leaving a land of red sandstone for one of granite. But before giving way to the harder stone and a consequent change in the landscape's character, the sandstone gives us one final glory of red with Sweetheart Abbey, inland from the eastern bounds of Galloway and by the mouth of the River Nith.

Sometimes the Old Bridge at Dumfries is called Devorguilla's Bridge, but that, if it existed, is more likely to have been an earlier wooden construction across the Nith. The Lady Devorguilla is, however, definitely associated with Sweetheart Abbey for she it was who caused it to be built in the 13th century in memory of her husband John Balliol, founder of Balliol College, Oxford. His heart, encased in ivory and silver, is buried beside Devorguilla under the High Altar of this 'Abbey of the Sweet Heart'.

Adjoining the Abbey, is the village of New Abbey. Here, the first hint of what will become evident here and there, the farther west we go — a tendency to paint housefronts in unorthodox colour schemes. We are coming in to artists' country you see, and the story goes that it all began some years ago when one of the artist community begged permission to paint the grey walls of the little kirk in his particular village. Not to paint a *picture* of it, but to apply a colour wash to its walls. In this way it was transformed into a warm glow of tangerine tone. The villagers were shocked; but grew used to the sight of it. And in time, contemplating the contrast of their own drab

façade — reached for a paint brush. . . .

Rockcliffe, by Dalbeattie (Dumfries & Galloway) The sands of Solway to the left, and inland by the coast road, some gardens boasting a palm tree or two — miniature though they may be — for this is the warmer Scotland where the Gulf Stream moves through the seas to the west. Beyond the fruitful fringe hinted at in the photograph, the Southern Uplands — a high land rival to that better known Highland of the Grampian range. Yet, this southern hill country, granite fashioned too, has a luxury of growth denied its sterner neighbour of the north.

The road ends at Rockcliffe and a way has to be retraced to continue on the main road west; but doing so is to deny the visitor an extra treat, for before continuing west a walk is recommended. A two-mile walk by pine wood and heather track with ever changing vistas of the Urr estuary and its sandbank and island below. And ahead, these higher hills . . . then down to Kippford and a world of yachts and little boats and a messing about in same; and talk in the pub with characters one meets in such places that glint with nautical souvenirs.

Now, back to Rockcliffe. Let's favour a flight of imagination and find a different way to the next stop at Dundrennan. And we'll go back in time too. . . . We are sailing, hugging the coast. This is smuggler country and note the odd names of rocks and inlets along the shore: we go west by Daft Anne Steps on Hestan Isle, Lot's Wife, Adam's Chair, Rascarrel Bay, Brock's Holes, Barlocco Bay, Dropping Craig and Spouty Dennans — to land at Abbey Burnfoot.

Dundrennan, by Kirkcudbright (Dumfries & Galloway) Inland two miles from Abbey Burnfoot, Dundrennan comes into view where Port Cheek and a mill are marked on the map — both reminders of the abbey's past. It is possible that small craft set off down the burn from Port Cheek to serve the bigger vessels (owned by the Cistercian monks of the abbey) waiting on the coast of Abbey Burnfoot for their trade with foreign countries. And the burn turned the mill wheel to grind the corn. The monks with laymen help, also farmed, bred horses and cattle and concerned themselves with the wool trade.

Dundrennan was the mother house of the Abbeys of Glenluce and of Sweetheart, being founded in 1142. After the Reformation when Dundrennan survived the threat of demolition, part of the abbey kirk served the parish until 1742. And through the ensuing years, before wiser council of comparatively recent times retained and preserved what remained, much of the stonework had gradually vanished. The grey village of Dundrennan nearby, was mostly built, it has been said, from the abbey fabric.

The abbey ruins, sombrely beautiful in this sequestered place, has surely its most poignant association with the past in the story of Mary, Queen of Scots, coming to Dundrennan. When her loyal army was defeated at Langside near Glasgow, Mary rode south and spent her last night in Scotland, at the abbey; and next morning journeyed to Abbey Burnfoot and crossed to England. Near Abbey Burnfoot, there's a Port Mary, and on the other side of Solway on the England shore, Maryport.

Kirkcudbright (Dumfries & Galloway) First, on how to pronounce Kirkcudbright. In so doing, its ancient origins are indicated. The Celts in the early Christian era, called it Caercuabrit and in time, spoken as 'Kirkcoobrie', this is still the phonetic form of the name.

Kirkcudbright, for long a seafaring community, has seen, among other stirring events, the assembling of the warriors of Galloway ready to sail against the Spanish Armada. Now the town is content to harbour smaller craft as shown in the photograph. And MacLellan's Castle makes a dramatic backcloth to the scene. No more than a backcloth now, but in the 16th century the MacLellan clan dominated the estuary of the River Dee between this castle and their other at Raeberry on the eastern corner of the bay.

In the following century Charles I created the MacLellan chief as Lord Kirkcudbright. Two hundred years on, and the peerage had become extinct with one of the last of the title reduced to keeping an ale-house in this royal burgh over which his ancestors had ruled in feudal times. A new lease of life in a different style came to Kirkcudbright in the early 1900s when the 'Kirkcudbright School' of artists blossomed forth. Their influence is maintained by their followers of today — in the little art galleries and exhibitions and in the manner in which the old streets, away from the commercialism at the riverside, show that a caring hand is at work to preserve these fine façades and alleyways and cobbled paths that delight the eye.

Author Dorothy Sayers was sufficiently intrigued by the town and its artists to feature both in her thriller *The Five Red Herrings*.

28

*Cardoness Castle, by Gatehouse of Fleet
(Dumfries & Galloway)* Cardoness, on the
shore road near Gatehouse-of-Fleet on the
river of that name, although no longer one
of the sentinels defending the Galloway
coast, has, like MacLellan's, stories to tell.
Here is one of them. It concerns a feud, after
the McCullochs had taken over the castle
from the Gordons.

Through the years, the Gordons nursed
their grievances; skirmishes and quarrels
kept the feud alive. Then in William Gordon
of the mansion of Bushybield in the wooded
country inland, they found a champion who
formally claimed, with the Law on his side,
Cardoness for the Gordons. This was near
the end of the 17th century. The Law
approached Sir Godfrey McCulloch. Sir
Godfrey, a man of violent tempers,
retaliated by arriving at Bushybield with a
loaded gun to demand a herd of cattle
which he insisted had been taken from the
McCulloch lands. One more of the many
quarrels marking the progress of the
families' history was sparked off; Sir
Godfrey lost control and shot and killed
Gordon.

McCulloch without delay fled south
across the Border. Some time later he
ventured back to Edinburgh to await news
of how events had developed at Cardoness
and while in the capital regularly attended
Sunday service — during which on one
memorable Sunday the sudden cry of 'Shut
the door, there's a murderer in the church'
startled the congregation and, no doubt also
the fugitive from justice. A Galloway man
happening to be seated near, had recog-
nised McCulloch. He was tried and executed
by guillotine in Edinburgh.

That guillotine, called 'The Maiden' is still
intact and on grim view in the National
Museum of Antiquities of Scotland in
Queen Street, Edinburgh.

Loch Trool, by Newton Stewart (Dumfries & Galloway) Time to leave the coast and explore inland — from Gatehouse-of-Fleet to the town of Newton Stewart, starting-off place for the Galloway Forest Park and Loch Trool and a wealth of forest trails. The Galloway Highlands, crowned by the 2,764ft high hill of Merrick, was once a battleground whose terrain suited the guerrilla warfare practised by Robert the Bruce and his band of patriots in the events preceding the Wars of Independence.

Existence for Bruce, the future King of Scots was made the more precarious since not all the chiefs of Galloway were for his cause. Like the Highland clans of the far north in later years — as also with the heads of the Border clans, these men of Galloway were far enough removed from authority to be a law unto themselves and less concerned with the attempts of Edward I of England 'The Hammer of the Scots' to dominate the country.

Thus Bruce, in these hills and forest wilds led a hunted life — sometimes with bloodhounds on his trail. It was in his hiding place above Loch Trool that he saw Sir Aylmer de Valance's troops advance for his capture — and contrived to send a torrent of huge boulders crashing down from the heights. Once more he had escaped. In a small wood nearby, tradition tells why the ancient trees have flourished so well: they have been fertilised at the roots for six centuries by English bones!

Isles of Whithorn (Dumfries & Galloway)
Stones that may in part have formed the walls of the first chapel at the dawn of Christianity here, now enclose pasture land.

That first chapel was St Ninian's who was born near the Isle when Galloway was briefly occupied by the Romans. And in time he journeyed to Rome where he was educated and ordained by the Pope. When he returned to his native coast, French masons who had accompanied him from where he had stayed at Tours on the way home, built the little chapel for him. Later he moved to Whithorn a few miles inland and established a monastic college for the training of prospective missionaries and the education of sons of Galloway chiefs.

The priory and museum at Whithorn remind one of these early times. And St Ninian, seeking isolation for meditation and prayer is said to have used the cave marked under the cliffs near Burrowhead. Burrowhead was a gunnery practice camp for the AA Command in the last war. Some readers may have belonged to the legions who came here as gunners in that time. I can tell them that on my last visit to the district, mushrooms were being grown commercially in the shadow of the former guard room; and holiday caravans were positioned where the guns had been.

There's a postscript to the above. In the 1950s in Edinburgh it happened that I met one of our former sergeants — armed now, with fishing rods and holiday luggage.

Where was he off to?

'Isle of Whithorn', he replied, 'I go there every year . . . it's the *peace* of the place.'

Portpatrick (Dumfries & Galloway) Portpatrick takes its name from a chapel dedicated to St Patrick, a contemporary of St Ninian. It seems proper that the patron saint of Ireland should be remembered here, since we are in sight of the coast of his country and in fact the Scottish mainland is almost at its nearest to Ireland here. Portpatrick, a holiday village now, was the main commercial port on this peninsula 100 years ago. But the harbour takes the full force of the western seas and attempts to improve its rock-bound approaches have never solved the navigation problems inherent on this coast in stormy weather. More sheltered, Stranraer has taken over as the principal port of the area; yet there was a time when at Portpatrick, as many as 20,000 head of cattle were annually landed from Ireland.

Some years ago, there was an unexpected brief revival of Portpatrick's days as a commercial harbour. My wife and I had come on holiday, and seeing the approach of a convoy of small vessels went down to see the catch unloaded. The 'catch' was eggs — thousands and thousands of dozens of eggs. Such unloading continued all week, adding other domestic comforts besides eggs — carpets for instance — by which time long distance lorries were at the quay, having come from as far as Kent. There was a country-wide dockers' strike at the time and Ireland was taking full advantage of Portpatrick's comparative seclusion and freedom from pickets.

That week ended in calm seas. The hotel laid on a dance for Saturday night. 'Will there be enough dancers to make it worth your while', we asked. 'Oh yes', explained the waiter, 'they'll come from Ireland too, you see — across the sea from Donaghadee.'

Castle Kennedy Gardens, Lochinch, by Stranraer (Dumfries & Galloway) Before the road north to the Carrick lands in Ayrshire, a final call in Galloway — to that pleasance of woods and waters where Castle Kennedy is mirrored from its sheltered position between the Black Loch and the White Loch. The castle was named after the Kennedy family who came south from Carrick in times long past and held sway over extensive lands here. As the old rhyme observes: ' 'Tween Wigtown and the Town of Ayr, Portpatrick and the River Cree, you shall not get a lodging there, except ye court a Kennedy'. Kennedys and Dalrymples were related through marriage. Dalrymple is the family name of the Earls of Stair whose power grew as the Kennedys' waned. Sir Walter Scott was an admirer of the Dalrymples and their good influence in the country. For example: in the 1640s, James Dalrymple a graduate of Glasgow University, became a distinguished soldier who, in his twenties as a professor of philosophy, would at times lecture to the students in his soldier's uniform. Today, the Galloway seat of the Earls of Stair, Premier Earls of Scotland, is Lochinch Castle by the White Loch.

Another soldier, the second Earl of Stair, commander of the Scots Greys in the 1800s liked to return to Castle Kennedy when not engaged in the European wars. And to him is attributed the initial care for the landscaping and cultivation of the lands by the lochs which laid the foundation for the garden splendour of today.

The Harbour at Maidens (Strathclyde)
Painted boats upon a painted ocean — the camera has caught a moment of suspended animation here; even the dog has momentarily paused for the picture. Maidens harbour, like other villages and small towns on the Ayrshire coast has an air of timelessness — of being the holiday place one remembers from childhood.

The road from Galloway enters the Carrick lands of Ayrshire at Glen App; then on to Glenapp Gardens, joining the coast at Ballantrae.

Robert Louis Stevenson's novel *The Master of Ballantrae* does not have any connection with the place. It may be that Stevenson liked the sound of the name as a good title word. He did once visit Ballantrae — and had cause to remember it, since the folk of the fishing village then, took violent exception to the bohemian style of his dress!

Farther north on the way to Maidens, is the town of Girvan, with sub aqua facilities to show that they can be modern-minded too. Ten miles out to sea from Girvan, Ailsa Craig, whose fine-grained granite did at one time supply most of the curling stones for the 'roarin' game'.

Maidens shares with adjoining Turnberry, the possible site where the beacon fire was lit to signal Robert Bruce, waiting on Arran, that the time had come to cross to the mainland and begin the fight for freedom.

One of the future king's titles was Earl of Carrick — a courtesy title borne by the Prince of Wales today.

It was here during World War 2 that many of the Beaufort and Beaufighter torpedo bomber crews learned their art — and never stopped arguing that Ailsa Craig was moving at five knots upwind.

Culzean Country Park (Strathclyde) The photograph shows Ailsa Craig on the horizon. Culzean Castle is at the heart of this country park of land and seascape.

Culzean (pronounced 'Culleen') in early times, was another stronghold of the Kennedys until at the end of the 18th century in the less warlike days of that time, it was redesigned as a stately home by Robert Adam for the 10th Earl of Cassillis (family name, Kennedy). During the period of its reconstruction, Adam also worked on the estate, designing the Home Farm buildings — now the Country Park Centre, with all facilities for the visitor.

In 1945 the National Trust for Scotland took over the castle and estate, presenting General Eisenhower with a private suite of rooms for his use, should he at any time visit Culzean. The General accepted this mark of appreciation for his services as Commander of the Allied Forces in Europe, and stayed here when he was in Scotland — once after he had been elected President.

I remember particularly the magnificent beech avenues here and that marvel of an oval staircase. As is so often the case, one detail remains vivid in mind among all the splendours on view. This was as a party of schoolchildren joined us from a village some distance away. They seemed a trifle awed by their surroundings until the guide picked up a delicately fashioned miniature music box and, for their special benefit, set the piece in motion. In the quiet of that great room a golden filigree of melody charmed the senses. I watched the little group of young scholars ... smiles slowly broadened their attentive faces. It was a moment to remember.

Dunure Castle (Strathclyde) Approaching Dunure from the south, one travels the 'electric brae'; the gradual slope downhill gives the impression of going uphill — and vice-versa coming the other way. The gradient is slight, but the illusion, an optical one, is due to the lay-out of the surrounding landscape.

Dunure Castle ruins provide the shoreline with a dramatic pictorial boost. Again, this was a Kennedy residence. Probably its defences were tested early in its history for this coast was attacked by the Norse rovers in their galleys before the final battle of Largs which rid the Scottish western seas of the Scandinavian menace.

In the middle of the 15th century, the Kennedy lust for land, caused the Commendator of Crossraguel Abbey to be slowly roasted over a fire in the Black Vault of the castle until he agreed to hand over to his tormentor the abbey lands!

Today, the little harbour and village of Dunure is a pleasant stop along the Ayrshire coastline. And its beach can be rewarding. One day my wife and I were beachcombing there, and found among other small stones, a dark brown wrinkled one looking like a miniature petrified potato.

When polished, it proved to be a cornelian agate and is now set in a ring. Later, we learned that the Dunure beach is a happy hunting ground for this modest amber-coloured gemstone.

44

*Auld Brig o' Doon and Burns Monument
(Strathclyde)* The poem *Tam o' Shanter*
was considered by Robert Burns to be his
masterpiece. The verses flowed from him in
a surge of inspiration while walking the
banks of the Nith at Dumfries. It tells this
tale. After drinking with his cronies following market day in Ayr, Tam sets out for
home on his grey mare, Meg, in a night of
black storm. At the Auld Kirk of Alloway he
is drawn to approach the ruined place by
sounds of unearthly revelry within. He finds
witches and warlocks dancing to a bagpipe
tune played by the Devil himself 'in shape o'
beast'. Tam's eye becomes concentrated on
Nannie, the young witch with an
abbreviated nightgown or 'cutty sark' (short
shirt) and his shout of acclamation at her
capers attracts her attention to him and
hardly had Tam time to turn Meg to the
road again when 'out the hellish legion
sallied' in pursuit.

Nearer and nearer to the Auld Brig over
the River Doon came the weird mob with
Nannie ahead of the rest. She it was who
grabbed the mare's tail as Tam reached the
keystone of the Brig. Tam was rescued by
the leap Meg gave, for witches cannot cross
running water — yet Nannie, swinging back
from that keystone and checking her
onward flight had managed to pull off
Meg's tail!

Burns ends in sermon fashion:

*When e'er to drink you are inclined,
Or cutty sarks run in your mind,
Think! ye may buy the joys o'er dear,
Remember Tam o' Shanter's mare.*

Largs (Strathclyde) Continuing north on the Ayrshire coast, holiday resorts increase in sophistication. The town of Largs strikes a balance by advertising itself as 'The family holiday resort with the Continental touch'.

This is where the Firth of Clyde narrows towards the river and Largs is finely situated to afford prospects of the islands across these narrowing seas, as viewed for instance from the hill on Douglas Park.

That same hill would have watchers of more serious intent in the late summer of 1263 when King Haco of Norway approached the mainland with his fleet of galleys. These Norsemen had harried the west coast and islands of Scotland from the days of the Viking longships and Haco had come to demand the islands by right of conquest: Alexander III of Scotland agreed to negotiate. He it was with his men who watched from the hill.

Alexander planned to make such negotiations last until the autumn's southwest gales would drive Haco's galleys to the shore where battle would be joined to the advantage of the men on land. And so it proved. Haco lost patience at the end of September and gave the signal for the advance. On the same day Alexander's prayers were answered in the form of a sudden beginning of the autumn gales which drove the galleys into the pounding surf in disarray. The battle lasted two days. Then Haco's much depleted fleet departed, never to return.

The Battle of Largs victory was one more step towards consolidating Scotland as a kingdom.

Glasgow — Tolbooth Steeple This tower, sometimes called the Cross Steeple, is all that remains of the great Tolbooth building, which, until a hundred years ago, was the heart of the business community. Earlier, at the end of the 18th century, Glasgow began its development into becoming the second city of the Empire. These were the days of the merchants who traded with the Americas — notably the 'Tobacco Lords' resplendent in their scarlet cloaks and tricorne hats as they paced the crown of the causeway with silver-knobbed canes.

Men of vision had seen the advantage of opening up the Clyde — of causing it to be dredged to let merchant sailing ships up river. From that, to building ships themselves — the beginning of the era of Glasgow's famed Clyde-built vessels. The tobacco men were replaced by the men of steel, culminating in recent history with the building of the *Queen Mary* and the *Queen Elizabeth II*.

It was estimated that 250,000 people were employed altogether in the building, fitting out and decoration of the *Queen Mary*; and that 200 outside industries were employed. For the machine-minded it may be of interest to know that the four sets of turbines contained 257,000 blades, each fitted and tested by hand. And the hull of the first Cunarder *Britannia* could have passed through one of the *Queen Mary* funnels with ease.

The *Queen Elizabeth II* is still with us and played her part in the Falklands conflict. Now she sails as a luxury liner. As Noel Coward once asked when a passenger on board: 'What time does this hotel get to New York?'.

Glasgow — Tron Steeple Here is another landmark — the Tron steeple with its archway a survival of the days of the piazzas — a feature of the Trongate in the 18th century. Note that colour has brightened its façade, an indication to the visitor that Glasgow, a city that lost so much of its fine architecture during the early industrial era is making the best of what has survived.

Stone-cleaning has caused the faces of smoke-grimed flats and tenements to glow again in the sun. Pedestrian precincts now give light and space where before were streets, traffic-crowded. The then necessary traffic-island refuges, have been replaced by beds of flowers.

And the buildings that must be visited include the cathedral named after Glasgow's founder and patron saint, St Mungo, with the vaulted crypt probably the most perfect example of its kind in Europe, the art gallery and museum at Kelvingrove, the Mitchell Theatre with the great Mitchell Library — and the crystal-like surprise appearance of the People's Palace Winter Gardens. But the principal jewel in Glasgow's newly burnished commercial crown is surely the Burrell Collection opened in 1983 by Queen Elizabeth.

Here, five miles west of the city centre and set in the Pollok Country Park, a gallery of glass — mostly glass — and light wood and fine-dressed pink sandstone contains the art collection of Sir William Burrell — a collection so vast that only part can be shown at one time. Here is something to please both connoisseur and ordinary visitor. Another pleasure for the ordinary visitor — a Glasgow facility in providing quick access to the Highlands. Loch Lomond for example is very much within call.

Stirling Castle (Central) To simplify complications attendant on Scotland's early history: Stirling Castle was the prize for Sir William Wallace, victor of the battle of Stirling Bridge in 1297 and for Bruce, victor of Bannockburn in 1314. (The statues of both men flank the entrance to Edinburgh Castle.)

Mention of Edinburgh reminds one to comment on the pictorial similarities of the two places. Both have a castle from which a street descends on a ridge; and viewed from Bridge of Allan to the north, Stirling's silhouette is reminiscent of Edinburgh's 'Royal Mile'.

Stirling Castle has the edge on Edinburgh in one sense. There is architectural refinement to be seen in the Stirling fortress which is less evident in the other; a smaller and more intimate royal residence was Stirling's too, with the domestic touch of a formal garden and other amenities. Mary, Queen of Scots, lived here in childhood.

Mary's father, James V, used the royal palace within the castle often in preference to Holyrood. And he appreciated the convenience of the underground passage at Stirling leading to the land below where he liked to mingle with his subjects incognito.

Mary's grandfather, James IV, was another unorthodox monarch fond of Stirling. He enjoyed the company of inventors of that age — like Damien, 'The French Leech', who attempted to turn base metal into gold and was encouraged to fly from the battlements with home-made wings. Fortunately a dunghill broke his fall. His excuse for failure: hen's feathers should not have been used.

Loch Arklett, Inversnaid (Central) This is Macgregor country. And at the loch's Lomondside end, Inversnaid, once the home of the most notorious Macgregor of all: Rob Roy.

The Macgregor clan had been outlawed by James VI following a battle with the Colquhouns after which a macabre procession of the widows of the slain Colquhouns set out for Stirling carrying their husbands' blood-stained shirts before them to plead for vengeance from the king. But in the ensuing years even feuds can fade and we find a Colquhoun employing Rob Roy to look after his cattle. This was when the Macgregor lands had been restored again and after John Campbell, 1st Earl of Breadlabane suggested that a 'Captain of the Watch' should be appointed to frustrate the activities of rustlers menacing the herds that were often a Highland chief's principal source of wealth. Unbelievably to some, Rob Roy Macgregor was appointed to the post, and became the instigator of a Highland 'protection racket', always with extra benefits to himself when possible. For example, should a body of cattle-thieves be stopped by Rob, if they could prove that the herd did not belong to one of Rob's employers, they were allowed to proceed... provided a percentage of the beasts — a small percentage, was left behind in the Macgregors' care.

Rob Roy, therefore, could be considered to be on the side of law and order... almost; but tolerating government authority from down south was another matter. A fort was built by Inversnaid to control the Highland clans. When completed, it existed for one day. The Macgregors blew a hole in the wall and burned the furnishings — 'which lit Glen Arklet from end to end'.

Loch Katrine, The Trossachs (Central) Sir Walter Scott rode the 20 miles from Glen Artney south of Comrie in Perthshire to the Trossachs at Loch Katrine to check on the route which would be featured in his epic poem *The Lady of the Lake*.

Scott wrote at length describing the scenic setting of this romance — wrote at length to the extent that he now tries the patience of the reader of today. The indubitable fact remains however, that Scott could tell a *story* and that his descriptions of the scenes in *The Lady of the Lake* did more to attract people to this lovely region of Scotland than any other writer before or since.

The hero of the piece — the Hunter, loses both stag and horse in the long chase, and becomes separated from his fellows. He himself is then lost.

There follows an account of his climbing a ladder-like arrangement of branches and tree-roots up a precipice, at that time forming a barrier to the loch (there was for long no road through to Katrine as now). Thus, when the Hunter wins to the heights, he looks down . . .

> *Where, gleaming with the setting sun,*
> *One burnished sheet of living gold.*
> *Loch Katrine lay beneath him roll'd*

Down now to the lochside, and in a last attempt to contact others of the hunt he sends the sound of his horn echoing across the wilds.

Mistaking the signal for another's, enter the lady of the lake in the person of the fair Ellen appearing in a small canoe from an islet on the loch . . . *A chieftain's daughter seem'd the maid.*

And there, we regret, we must leave the reader. . . .

Glen Ample Falls, Lochearnhead (Central)
At the west end of Loch Earn and on the south side of the loch, this sylvan scene in the little glen named, contrariwise, Ample.

Scotland's waterfalls vary from one in the far and inaccessible northwest with a fall rivalling Niagara in height (not, of course, in width) — to delectable miniatures like the Falls of Bruar off the A9 in the Atholl country. Some of the falls have been tamed, following operations by the Scottish Hydro Electric Board — the falls of Tummel near Pitlochry, for instance. Others, no more than burns or little streams gain

distinction by happening to leap from high — as the 'Grey Mare's Tail' spilling downhill 200ft near Moffat in the Borders does. It is presumably named after Meg the grey mare who lost her tail in Burns's poem *Tam o' Shanter* already commented on.

Loch Earn itself is notable for its being the first stretch of loch in Scotland to welcome the water skiers. Five miles east of the other end of the loch, Comrie (from whose adjacent Glen Artney began the hunters' chase in *The Lady of the Lake*) should be mentioned in passing since it houses the Museum of Scottish Tartans.

Glencoe (Highland) Glencoe will for ever be associated with the Massacre of 1692. Today, no grimmer mountain background could be devised for the tragedy than those dark frowning heights. Imagination inclines one to create a brooding atmosphere about the glen. And I was aware of this when setting out to climb between the two peaks shown in the photograph, during a solo teenage Highland hike long ago.

It is important to remark the weather of that day. The sky was a still haze of sulphureous gloom, prelude as it happened, to a thunderstorm next day. There was not a breath of wind, even on the heights. In time, finding myself stuck on a ledge of rock and unable to rise farther or retreat with any comfort, I could at least see over the top edge to a bald plateau-like surface of stones shattered by centuries of frost and, in that unhappy position spend some time contemplating the next move — if any. . . .

Across the plateau and coming from right to left, two men in mountaineering gear with old-style studded boots. They were smiling and talking, stumping across that barren floor of stone only some 30 yards away. Should I call for help? The sudden decision not to, was prompted by a curious chill of fear which sent me slithering down that rock face then on to the steep long grass and mossy slopes and eventually in relief, to the haven of the road — for in that still windless air above, the two men had been talking, laughing and striding across a hard stone way — yet, *not one sound had come from them!*

62   Had I seen two ghosts — in daylight?

The Old Bridge of Dee, Invercauld (Grampian) This is a good example of how a practical construction built without any conscious thought of being artistic, evolves into a work of art. This beauty of a bridge, finished in 1752, of which the central arch is shown here, was also built for a very practical reason so far as the Government of the time was concerned — to carry the new military road across the river.

After the Jacobite Rising of 1745, it was decided to open up the Highlands by building proper roads so that movement of military personnel would be facilitated and thus be better able to keep the Highlanders under control. Roads that would also link with forts: Fort William for example, named after the king associated with the Glencoe story; and Fort George built in 1748.

It was a military man who got the task of supervising the making of these roads and bridge crossings — the Irish General, George Wade. And from that work began the Ordnance Survey, whose directors of today, still have associations with the Army.

Many of our present Highland roads have General Wade to thank for the initial planning. The best known bridge connected with the General, is Wade's bridge at Aberfeldy across the Tay. And south of that in the Sma' Glen towards Crieff, although the Wade road in that region has long vanished, its route is still indicated at one part by a parallel line of boulders rolled out of the way by the soldiers who cleared the required passage through.

Craigievar Castle (Grampian) Craigievar, between the Rivers Dee and Don and rising near the summit of a thousand-foot hill, looks west to where the farmer and the forester have tamed the once wild land; and small ponies, domesticated, browse in a meadow by the castle grounds.

As one approaches along the drive, this great tower-house matches in elegance the tall trees surrounding it. Inside, panelled rooms are seen as an ever-ascending panorama in the vertical — there are six storeys — each revealing some new interior of a warm intimacy in this baronial masterpiece completed by Laird William Forbes in 1626.

This Forbes was a merchant, which made something of a change in these days when the warrior's lance was easier come by than a laird with a ledger.

William's descendant, the Red Sir John was less of a laird than a man cast in the mould of a lord of earlier times — sitting in the great hall of Craigievar, dispensing justice in the feudal manner — which he did. Small crimes like 'louping (leaping) and breaking down dykes' meant a fine of 40 shillings. For a man who threw another man's wife to the ground — 'blooding her nose and taking up her clothes and belting her' — the fine was £50, and £4 to pay to the husband and wife for the indignity suffered.

To end on a more dignified note: consider that great hall. It is a splendour of refinement in plaster work — a vaulted chamber heraldically decorated, all crowned above the fireplace with a superb royal arms with the Scottish unicorn in pride of place.

Crathes Castle (Grampian) Some years ago, approaching the little town of Banchory on Deeside, and seeing across the river the Castle of Crathes, I was so impressed that I contrived to be given permission from the owner, the late Sir James Burnett of Leys to make a sketch of what was at that time, his private residence. My wife and I remember well that day of pale sunshine and the woodland peace surrounding the Castle; and of how, after introducing themselves, Sir James and Lady Burnett left us in sole occupation of the lovely walled gardens and flower-bordered pathways. That was after he had first approved the angle I had chosen for the drawing of this building which, like Craigievar, shows the tower-style peculiar to Scotland where the turrets, once built for defence, were retained in the less warlike days of the early 17th century and became extended and decorated as a distinctive feature of these splendid houses of the northeast.

In 1961, Sir James handed over Crathes Castle and nearly 600 acres of land to the National Trust for Scotland. Visitors can now see not only the interior of its painted ceilings and the woodwork of the gallery, among other treasures, but follow the nature trail through the 400 acres of woodland surrounding the castle.

Mentioned in the booklet on the trail is a 'Ginkgo' tree, an ancient species which apparently flourished over 50 million years ago. The trail passes the old oak wood of Crathes; probably the descendants of the wood which grew here when Robert the Bruce presented the land to the first Burnett of Leys.

Aberdeen Harbour Strange superstructures, streamlined sterns, colours of strident orange and peacock blue, new names like *Oil Mariner* on the bows — we refer, of course, to the modern sea rovers who take their rainbow-hued craft into the grey wastes of Scotland's eastern seas from Aberdeen harbour. Aberdeen is now accustomed to the new faces — Norwegian and American among them. And accustomed to the new ways of life in this Granite City of the northeast which has become the Oil Capital of Europe. Where before, in the old-established hotels, business men of sober garb would occupy the lounge, now younger men wearing patched jeans and a faintly piratical air are inclined to be in the ascendant.

Yet, the douce natives of the city have not themselves changed. Aberdeen continues to be a major fishing port and claims to have a history of a flourishing merchant community earlier than either Edinburgh or Glasgow.

Add to that, Aberdeen, not only having to contend in the past with would-be conquerors from the south but with the added menace of Highlanders from the west — as with one, Donald, Lord of the Western Isles who advanced to pillage the town in 1411 and was met and routed by a force including the townsfolk themselves. All of which has bred a race of northeastern Scots with something of the granite in their natures. But dour? No. Let it be noted for example, that 250,000 roses from an Aberdeen nursery were handed out free to shoppers in the city last summer — a move by traders to add pleasure to purchasing.

King's College, Aberdeen To leave Aberdeen without seeing the 'Auld Toon' is to miss a pictorial and architectural treat. Whether you like granite rough-dressed or polished smooth, both examples are on display. But before leaving the 'New' Town have a look at 'Provost Ross's' house as an example of granite rough-dressed at its best — then contemplate the Mitchell Tower of Marischal College... too well-dressed? And see at the east end of Aberdeen's mile-long Union Street, the Market Cross modelled on the old Edinburgh Cross.

Now for the 'Auld Toon' or, Old Aberdeen. And into University land under James IV's crown tower of King's College. Savour the quiet paved ways of the Chanonry to St Macher's Cathedral whose ceiling of panelled oak is embellished with heraldic shields of the kings of Europe, dignitaries of the Church and the arms of the monarchs and nobles of Scotland.

So to the River Don and the Brig of Balgownie. Compared to the River Dee which in winter can send down ice floes from Braemar, the Don is placid, more pastoral. The sparkle of this stream where it finds its way through the fields of the Howe of Alford in the Craigievar country is stilled at Balgownie as if the waters were daunted and afraid to join with the fierce ocean tides beyond, but in the stillness, reflect in their dark depths, the single sweet arch of the bridge.

A good place this, to say goodbye to Aberdeen. On the north side of the Balgownie arch, a line of cottages with rough-hewn stone walls compact and comfortable under the soft orange-red of old pantiles. Is this a place where Old Granite will for ever resist and never mix with New Oil?

Crovie (Grampian) This is a fine example of the small fishing villages of the northeast coast running west towards the Moray Firth. Characteristically, the houses huddled under the cliff, present their gable to the sea. Crovie is now in a conservation area and many of the cottages are owned by holiday weekenders. Much of the fishing industry in this region today is centred on the bigger ports like Fraserburgh.

Other coastal villages in this district worth a visit are Pennan just east of Crovie and Rosehearty five miles east of Pennan. In the other direction, Whitehills 10 miles west of Crovie and a mile or two west of that, Portsoy. Portsoy marble is now fashioned into souvenirs. Anyone acquiring such a souvenir should know that this green marble formed fireplaces in the Versailles of Louis XIV. While in the vicinity, Duff House and the Georgian domestic architecture of the town of Banff are worth seeing.

To revert to the villages: these attract artists for their pictorial qualities, but painting impressions of the restless seas itself is another matter. I am reminded of the late Joan Eardley in the forefront of Scottish painters in recent times. She lived at Catterline a fishing village on the east coast of Aberdeen. And a fisherman there once told me: 'Sometimes when it was too rough for the boats to go out, she'd be down at the beach there wi'' her easel weighted and tied to the rocks — and herself wi' paint and palette, facin' the big waves comin' roarin' in'.

Stonehaven (Grampian) Coming down the east coast, first stop after Aberdeen — Stonehaven — more of a holiday resort than a fishing port now. It shares with Aberdeen the recreational peculiarity of 'Outdoor Draughts' — the game, not the bracing air. Imagine a draughts board of stone set into the pavement with each square big enough to take draughts the size of soup plates, with a ring inset in the centre. The competitors then stand or sit, armed with a pole with a hook on its end for moving the draughts to the chosen square.

Something more exciting was going on, once, two miles south of Dunnottar Castle in the time of Cromwell who happened to be besieging this fortress to where the Regalia had been hurried from Edinburgh Castle for safety — knowing Cromwell's opinions of 'baubles' sacred or otherwise. With only a token force inside Dunnottar, it was merely a matter of time before occupation by the besiegers. Meantime, Mrs Grainger, wife of the minister of Kinneff kirk seven miles south, had permission during the siege to visit the governor's wife in Dunnottar who passed the time spinning flax. Most days Mrs Grainger would ride up the coast with her maid alongside and sometimes take away cloth that had been spun.

On one occasion, Mrs Grainger left with the Crown of the Regalia tied around her waist under her ample skirts and the Sword of State and Sceptre inside the bolt of cloth carried on the maid's back. The Regalia were buried in Kinneff kirk, where they remained until they were returned to Edinburgh on the restoration of the monarchy nine years later.

Boddin Point, Lunan Bay (Tayside) Boddin Point is two miles south of Montrose. In the photograph, rusted anchors, fishing nets and a lime kiln, illustrating — an ancient seagoing tradition — a present day fishing industry — and a monument to the days when lime first fertilised the now rich agricultural acres inland from Montrose.

Montrose, with its four miles of sand for the holidaymaker and a High Street that is the architectural pride of the place, unlike any other town in Scotland, boasts a 'lagoon'. This two mile wide stretch of water where the River Esk spreads itself before meeting with the sea, has become a sanctuary for all manner of wildfowl.

As with all seaports merchant-trading in the earlier days of sail, Montrose suffered from pirates. One of the most enterprising was a Dutchman who captured a vessel coming north from Ipswich and took his prize into Montrose where he advertised to the sea-going fraternity that he was about to organise a sale. The wise ones of Montrose itself steered clear of this marketing of another man's goods, but buyers came from St Andrews and as far as Leith near Edinburgh. The cargo of wheat, rye and malt was sold off; then the sails, masts and cables. Repercussions followed in authorities' attempt to recover the property sold so illegally, but the Dutchman himself had long vanished.

To revert to the present time: at each end of Lunan Bay, rocks of a 'surrealist' cast, show Nature in her mood as abstract sculptress. And at Boddin Point and nearby Ferryden semi-precious stones are worth searching for.

Arbroath (Tayside) While some folks are said to have fairies at the bottom of their garden, Arbroath folk have 'smokies'. Many of the fishing community smoke their catch of haddock in sheds at the bottom of their garden plots and Arbroath smokies are a Scots dish that in its way is just as much appreciated as smoked salmon.

Here, as at every harbour, seagulls yell a welcome; and another sound with a captivating drone draws one to the fish salesman auctioning the catches. To the uninitiated ear it sounds just like — 'Burly girlie, burly girlie, burly girlie *fifteen*, burly girlie, burly girlie, burly girlie *seventeen* . . .' and so on; while a static group around him stare at the fish and the fish stare back.

In the busy sea-breezed streets of Arbroath, every now and then one glimpses the round window space, high on the gable end of the abbey's south transept, where once the monks placed a lantern to guide the seamen home. It was to this abbey some years ago that the young men brought the Stone of Destiny or Coronation Stone which they had taken from under the Coronation seat in Westminster Abbey. And, draped in the national flag of Scotland — the St Andrew's Cross, left it at the site of the high altar where the Declaration of Independence was made over 600 years ago — the Declaration ending with the words: 'It is not for glory or riches that we fight, but for freedom alone, which no good man gives up but with his life'.

And even farther back in history, at St Vigean's church near the town, and in a wayside cottage, there is a unique collection of Early Christian stones and tablets, Pictish carved.

Tay Road Bridge to Dundee (Fife) One of Dundee's signs of moving with the times, this road bridge across the River Tay.

Dundee, the fourth city of Scotland and the second industrially, has long been defined by the popular phrase 'the home of jam, jute and journalism'. Jam, in its form as marmalade, may not be the personal product it once was; and jute is more symbolic of the greater days in Victorian times; but journalism continues triumphant in the presence of the HQ at the centre of the city, of one of the longest established and most successful publishing houses in Britain.

The University of Dundee was created in one sense, from jute, that raw fibre from India, processed in the mills here, for the fortune of the Baxter family of jute fame founded the University College in 1881. It received university status in 1967.

An elderly relative once recalled to me his memory of watching the sailing ships coming up the river with their jute cargoes when a boy. And also the night of the Tay Bridge Disaster of December 1897 when the driver of a passenger train, unaware that the central section of the railway bridge had collapsed into the Tay, began the fatal crossing. Today, its successor, upstream from the road bridge, is one of the longest railway bridges in the world.

Dundee is backed by the Sidlaw hills and the lands of Angus — and Glamis Castle is one of the places of interest to visit in that fertile rolling plain north of the city.

82

St Andrews (Fife) From the harbour, the photograph shows the cathedral ruins, and left, St Rule's Tower. Thomas Carlyle put it all in a nutshell when he said: 'A grand place, St Andrews. You have there the essence of all the antiquity of Scotland, in good clean condition'. And in the Kate Kennedy procession each April one has all the essence of its history in pageant form. Kate, a medieval notoriety, rides in a carriage, her modern representative always being a first-year male student. The parade leaves St Salvator's College (founded by her uncle Bishop Kennedy in the early 15th century) led by the figure of St Andrew carrying the saltire cross of his martydom which now forms the national flag. (It was to this coastal region that St Rule and his followers came with the relics, the bones of St Andrew, in the 4th century.)

Famous figures of Town and Gown walk or ride in the pageant, including James Wilson a local boy who made good, graduating from the university, then emigrating to America where in time he was one of the principals in setting down the Constitution of the United States.

My own memories of St Andrews centre on the beauty of the grey colleges graced with old trees, all contrasting favourably with the fleeting glimpse of a red-gowned student. And on a course of this Royal and Ancient home of golf, watching and wondering why the golfer about to tee-off paused . . . then seeing why, as a procession crossed the fairway — a file of fat-cheeked donkeys on their way to their day's work on the holiday beach.

84

Pittenweem (Fife) The East Neuk of Fife cherishes, in the Firth of Forth part of its arrow-headed coastline of only 10 miles, as many picturesque corners of harbours and housing of crow-stepped gables and red pantiled roofs, to keep a photographer or artist happy for long enough. And all livened by the fisher folk — although they are not always easy to get to know.

In Pittenweem, one of the busiest ports, I once tried to get a 'story' out of a hardy old-timer. He chose not to co-operate: 'Nah, nah, aw' best forgotten.' was his refrain — yet went on — 'Out there in the Firth in 1941 held at pistol point, got away, never mind how — nah it was not a submarine; anyway, best forgotten... and I've been washed over the side o' the boat and washed back into the same boat in one night o' storm, but nah, nah, best forgotten...'

The word Pitten*weem* in its final syllable derives from an ancient word meaning cave — and a saint's cave — St Fillan's some say, although St Adrian is the patron saint of the burgh, is still on view. One opens a door in a rock face and enters the cavern where a light burns by a simple altar piece. But it is the charm of the old houses and the life of the fishmarket which attracts most of the visitors.

Pittenweem had royal associations; with Charles II for one. It was a shipowner of the burgh who, loyal to the king, took him to France in 1651 after his defeat at the battle of Worcester. That shipmaster's house, 'The Giles', is one of the showpiece restorations by the harbour today.

Falkland Palace (Fife) The little burgh of Falkland at the heart of the 'kingdom' of Fife, is dominated by the royal palace, a favourite residence when royalty were away from the cares of State — although the gatehouse of the palace shown here, must have always been a reminder of Holyrood.

Falkland (falcon land) was a popular hunting seat with the Stuarts, among others, with James V who caused the palace to be completed in its present form. It was also favoured by his wife, Mary of Guise, mother of Mary, Queen of Scots. Apart from the beauty of the stonework, the carvings, the chapel, the heraldic refinements which have survived a Cromwellian assault and occupation at one time by Rob Roy and his clansmen, there is a fine spread of palace garden in pleasing contrast to the old grey walls.

The burgh itself is worth looking at too. The ancient cobbled 'wynds' and the indication of a past prosperity in the gilded plaques on house fronts — and a memorial or two to distinguished sons of the burgh. One man who merits particular attention and a native of Falkland, is Richard Cameron, the Covenanter.

When Charles II returned from exile, he attempted to impose the Episcopal faith on all Scotland, thus outlawing the Presbyterians. They found a champion in Cameron who actually challenged the king's forces to fight — which they did. Cameron was killed in battle leading a fervid band of followers to whom he was now a martyr. From them, the Convenanting army stemmed and from that army developed one of Scotland's famous infantry regiments — The Cameronians.

88

Lochleven, Kinross (Fife) The loch has two islands and is famed for its trout. What surely catches the imagination of the visitor however is the smaller island — Castle Island, where Mary, Queen of Scots was imprisoned and from where she made a daring escape in a final bid for freedom after being forced to abdicate in favour of her son.

Mary's loyal page, Willie Douglas, attended her, and, since there was no possibility of the queen leaving the island, she was not closely guarded.

Willie the page, acquired the castle key. One version tells how at supper one evening when Mary was dining with the governor, Willie noticed the key lying on the table and covered it with a napkin, hoping that the governor in absentmindedness would forget to collect it — as he did — when rising from the table.

Later that night Mary and her faithful page stole down to the water's edge having locked the castle gate from without to delay any pursuit, and thrown the key into the loch. Then they set out in a small rowing boat for the shore near the town of Kinross. . . .

Today, a small motor launch repeats that journey in reverse when taking visitors across to the island. When I was last there, the guide talked as if he had known Mary. He showed me the path she took round to the little chapel. He made her presence come alive again.

Some years ago a great key was found in the loch. It may have been the one that Willie threw away when they set out across the water?

Dunfermline Palace (Fife) The photograph shows the abbey with part of the fabric of the former palace in the foreground. The nave of Dunfermline Abbey reminds one of the nave of Durham. Both have great pillars scored in the Norman geometrical pattern.

The abbey, the first in Scotland, was founded by Queen Margaret who married the Scottish king, Malcolm III. She had arrived as a refugee in a small boat, beaching on the north side of the Forth at a place now called St Margaret's Hope between the Forth rail and road bridges. Margaret brought a civilising influence to Scotland in the latter part of the 11th century. One of Edinburgh's oldest buildings, the chapel in the Castle, is named after Margaret. It was in Edinburgh that she died, a few days after her husband was killed in battle at Alnwick. Her body was taken to Dunfermline for burial where, in time, seven Scottish kings were to be laid to rest.

Margaret had interesting family associations. She was a cousin of Stephen's queen — the Stephen who was Hungary's legendary king mentioned in the carol *Good King Wenceslas*. In time, Stephen was made a saint, as was Margaret, canonised in 1249.

Influences for good have not been confined to royalty here. Andrew Carnegie, born in Dunfermline, became a millionaire and gave his town the charming Pittencrieff Glen set out below the abbey — one of his many endowments.

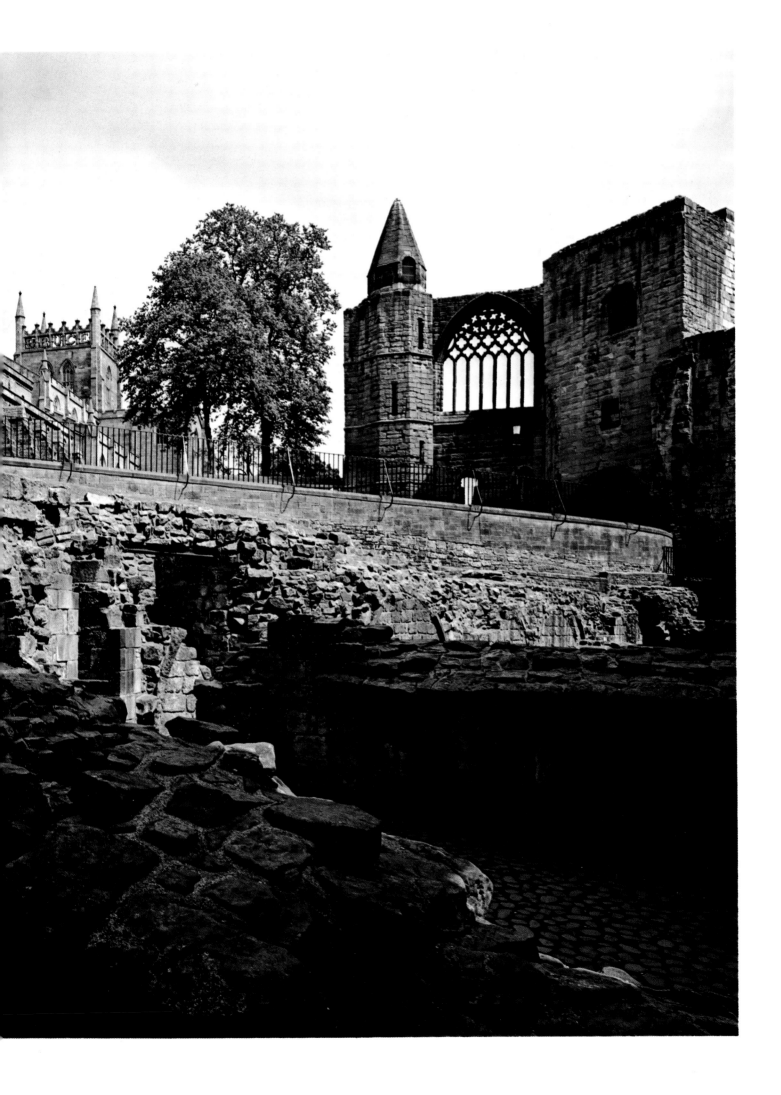

Culross (Fife) Considering its proximity to the River Forth and thus open to visits in the old days from pirates and others bent on destruction, that Culross (pronounced 'Kooross') has survived as probably the most complete example of what a small Scots town of the 16th and 17th centuries looked like, is something of a miracle.

The photograph shows at right, the tall building known as The Study — formerly the home of one, Bishop Leighton. And beyond, the ogee-shaped roof top of the Tolbooth under which witches and other enemies of law and order were held. Culross (a few miles west of Dunfermline) also has a 'palace' — a show-piece now, but in its heyday, the mansion of a coalmine owner.

King James VI once toured a mine here, descending a mainland shaft, but coming up to ground level through a shaft — to his surprise — in the centre of an islet offshore. James, ever apprehensive of his well being, with visions of kidnapping or worse, on his mind, yelled 'Treason'! All is quiet now in Culross — a domestic pleasance, where once the quays were alive with merchant ships from the Continent and the close-set walls echoed to the iron-worker's hammer.

Some years ago I was privileged to meet an elderly lady here with an unusual name. Mrs Scotland, a widow, told me; 'My man used to light all the oil lamps in the streets, and weed between the cobbles'. A prelude to the care now given by the National Trust for Scotland.

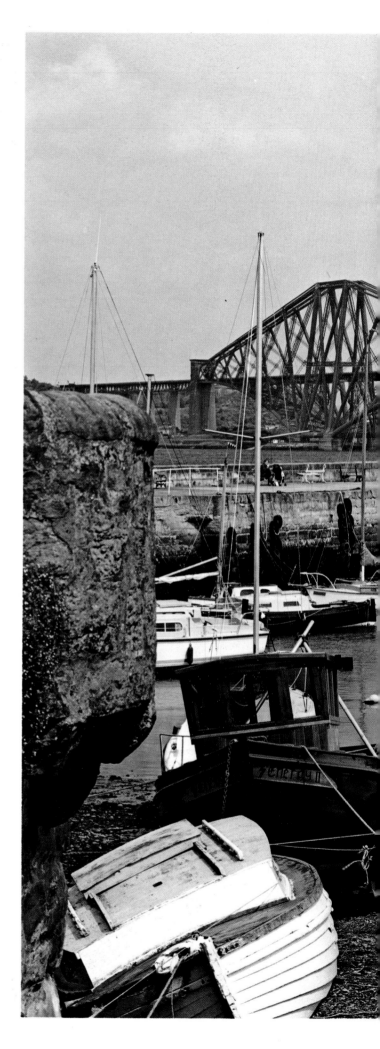

The Forth Railway Bridge, Queensferry (Lothian) Much has been written about the Forth Rail Bridge during its lifetime which began in 1890, less about its 'keystone' — the little island of Inchgarvie — huddling modestly under the great girders and noticed by few. Yet, without its existence, life would have been more difficult for the designers and for the host of workmen employed in the bridge's construction.

Inchgarvie, less of an island than a large rock, had been fortified to protect shipping from 'pirates and rovers' in times past and its old castle came in useful again when it — 'was roofed in and modernised, affording accommodation for the workmen. Various minor shops, sheds and smithies were also erected.'

The island's underwater rock was to hold four of the huge supporting piers and while the casing for these were being prepared 80ft below the surface workmen were astonished to see salmon leaping into the chamber. The commotion in the water outside caused when compressed air left the casing or chamber, attracted the fish whose instinct was to fight their way up the 'cascade'.

Everyone has heard that the painting of the Forth Bridge is an ever-ending job. Not so many may know that a man in a boat is tethered below the bridge under wherever the painters are working on the chance that there may be a fall. The last boatman life-saver I heard of passed the time repairing clocks and watches.

Linlithgow Palace (Lothian) The building, begun in the 15th century, grew into what Sir John Stirling-Maxwell, an authority on the subject, called 'the most imposing residence of the Scots kings'. With such sculptured magnificences remaining and such height of ancient walls, the palace could hardly be called a ruin. The stone gateway adorned with the heraldic orders of knighthood is virtually intact — as is the decorated fireplace in the Great Hall — a fireplace at least 24ft wide.

James IV who was killed at the battle of Flodden in 1513 did much to improve Linlithgow Palace, but it reached its full splendour in the reign of his son James V who built the fountain in the Inner Close, since copied in much of its detail for the one made for the forecourt at Holyrood. One of the last residents in the palace was Prince Charles Edward Stewart on which occasion, 'the fountain ran with wine'.

An enterprising guide some years ago when taking a party of schoolchildren round the palace, had contrived to introduce previously some purple-red liquid dye into the fountain's interior piping. When he told the scholars of the fountain running with wine, he then, with a fine sense of theatre, switched the waters on. . . .

In the photograph, note the curious top to the tower of the 15th century St Michael's kirk. Originally it had a crown to the tower but that had long vanished and a modern one was created by a sculptor of today. It was lowered on by helicopter — an ingenuity which would have surely delighted James IV who gave the original crown to the kirk and was ever a man keen on invention and experiment.

Gladstone's Land, Edinburgh A 'land' means a building in this instance. Old Edinburgh is made up in most part by these lands. This one is in the Lawnmarket, the section of the Royal Mile between the High Street and Castlehill. To confuse the visitor further, the Lawnmarket's original name was 'Landmarket' — the market used by traders from outside of the town — the *landward* side. William Gledstane (Gladstone) came from Kirkcudbright and bought the building early in the 1600s and set about reconstructing the property. He became landlord to a democratic collection of tenants, at one time including a minister of religion, a merchant, a knight, and an officer of the Town Guild.

Gladstone probably occupied with his wife the third of the six floors. This is suggested by there being a 'gled' (Scots word for a kite or hawk) on that third-floor painted ceiling. And a gilded kite is now the latest sign to adorn the front of the house.

In the 1930s Gladstone's Land awaited the demolisher as approved by an unimaginative local authority of the time. A Miss Helen Harrison, more heritage-minded, had other ideas. She bought the building and handed it over to the National Trust for Scotland. A shop front was removed and revealed the original arches, the windows were properly paned and the oak shutter boards have been reintroduced on the windows of the lower floors. Now, the house brings Edinburgh of the 17th century alive again — and, as Sir James Barrie said referring to another Scottish place — ''it likes to be visited.'

Whitehorse Close, Edinburgh As with Gladstone's Land, a worthy restoration. Whitehorse Close is now residential. At one time it was a coaching inn. The wooden balconies flanking a courtyard once bustling with activity as travellers prepared to leave, were taken down when the close was repaved, but the arched shelters for the coaches — presumably the road level was lower in the 18th century — are still there at the rear of the building.

In the early days of such travel, people often made their wills before setting out and, taking solemn farewell of their friends, asked to be prayed for in the churches.

Early in the 18th century, organisation of travel was improving. Apart from Whitehorse Close there was at least one other hostelry at that time catering for travellers to London. Here is its advertisements:-

> 'The Edinburgh and London Stage Coach begins on Monday 13 October 1712. All that desire . . . let them repair to the Coach and Horses at the head of the Canongate every Saturday, or the Black Swan in Holborn every other Monday at both of which they may be received in a coach which performs the whole journey in thirteen days without stoppage (if God permits) having eighty able horses.'

Another inn (or the same as above, renamed?) is commemorated in a plaque on the east side of St Mary's Street at the head of the Canongate in Boyd's Close. Here in 1773, Dr Johnson arrived and put up at the inn from where he sent this succinct note:- *"Saturday night*. Mr Johnson sends his compliments to Mr Boswell being just arrived at Boyd's.'

Edinburgh from Calton Hill Foreground left, the memorial to Professor Dugald Stewart, a friend of Robert Burns. Looking down, Princes Street lies like a sword blade separating the Old Town (left) from the New.

From this vantage point a prospect round all points of the compass is available — especially if one ascends the Nelson column — with Ben Lomond looking over the horizon to the northwest and seaward, North Berwick Law to the east.

Through the years Calton hill has become a magnet for monuments among which is included the brass cannon ranged on Princes Street. It was cast about 1600 to the order of a Count de Silva during Spain's occupation of Portugal. An inscription in Burmese along its barrel records the capture of the gun by that country during the campaigns in the East Indies. Later, it was taken by the British at Mandalay in 1886 and presented to Edinburgh in the same year.

Apart from monuments, the observatory deserves notice. Since the Royal Observatory was established on Blackford hill, the Calton one decreased in importance — until it was taken over by the Astronomical Society of Edinburgh, run by enthusiastic amateurs. An interesting enterprise is due to be introduced here — *Camera Lucida*. The installation of this wonder camera is promised for the summer of 1984. No details on its method of functioning are to hand at the moment of writing, hence the slight air of mystery surrounding this promised new amenity in which audio-visual aids and cinema film will be incorporated, considerably enhancing the viewing facilities from the hill.

North Berwick, Lothian A holiday resort where the red sandstone of East Lothian — the colourful county, predominates. The photograph shows Berwick Law in the background. Its summit, decorated with the jawbones of a whale, is a good place from which to point out some of the attractions around.

Out to sea, the Bass Rock, home of an ever-vocal multitude of gannets (solan geese) and other seabirds; also in its day, 'home' in the 17th century to Covenanters imprisoned there — as it was for Jacobite adherents in Prince Charlie's cause, later. The Jacobites fared better, for they overcame their guards and made the Bass Rock their own — 'colonised' it — with a bit of piracy on the side to help with supplies and with support from sympathisers on the mainland. And they had a cannon, too.

Just over two miles east of Berwick Law, Tantallon Castle, red on its red cliff rock — a stronghold of the Douglases, ever a thorn in the side of Scottish kings. And farther along the coast here, Seacliff of the wide sandy bay and a little harbour hewn from the solid rock.

Two miles west of the Law, Dirleton, considered to be well in the running as Scotland's prettiest village, with a generous village green and an ancient castle in whose grounds a bowling green and garden are set, with the latter's wide herbaceous border surely a quarter of a mile long if stretched out in one line?

Finally, back to the coast here — to Yellowcraigs Nature Trail where we are in Robert Louis Stevenson country. Scenes in his novel *Catriona*, the sequel to *Kidnapped* take place here.

Dunbar Castle Ruins, Lothian This photograph shows the ruins of Dunbar Castle which seem to leap gaps in the coastal cliff and generally give one the impression as one wanders around it, that here must have been a particularly formidable defence work in its day. Certainly an English force who attempted to capture it in 1339 during Scotland's 'Wars of Independence' found this was so when 'Black Agnes', Countess of Dunbar, was able, in her husband's absence, to hold out with her band of henchmen for over six weeks.

One other point about the castle ruins: they have become a haven for seabirds including a colony of kittiwakes.

The huge harbours of Dunbar are given over mainly to the holiday maker with the fishing industry now subdued. The harbours are of interest to anyone keen on domestic architecture for here some of the buildings have been ingeniously adapted and transformed into modern flats. Of the older buildings, the Town House in the High Street and The Barracks (once the great mansion of Lauderdale House) are worth attention.

Dunbar is today at the centre of two wildly diverging features. To the southeast of the town, the controversial Torness Nuclear Power Station. To the west, the John Muir Country Park — a miniature national park at Bellhaven sands and named after a native of Dunbar who became a world-famous botanist and conservationist, travelling the great wildernesses of America for material for his writings and for rare botanical treasures.

108

St Abbs (Borders) On a 25 mile-stretch of this coast there are seven lifeboat and coastguard stations. Rough cliff country this, and never rougher than at Fast Castle just up the coast from St Abbs. The castle, or what remains of it, is confined on a needle of rock out from the main cliff. To win to Fast Castle and its rock top not much wider than between the wickets on a cricket pitch, one crosses a narrow neck of turf linked with the mainland by a 'gangway' chain-bordered on either side . . . for safety.

As far back as the 15th century, this castle was being fought over by the Scots and the English. And treasure is reputed to be hidden in its craggy depths. Last time I was there, the remains of a battered hulk of a cargo steamer was pinned to the rocks below the cliffs to the south — this is a grim but highly adventure-charged region of Berwickshire.

All here was good smuggling country; St Abbs itself, no exception. The same at Eyemouth down the coast. There, it is noticeable that some of the houses have doors in odd places and gables facing where house fronts should be — all to facilitate in the old days, a quick passage in avoiding the Law — or escape from it. Or to be able to slip across the Border into England — which is what our cameraman could be considered to be doing, now that, with this photograph, he has completed the series and come to journey's end.

List of Plates

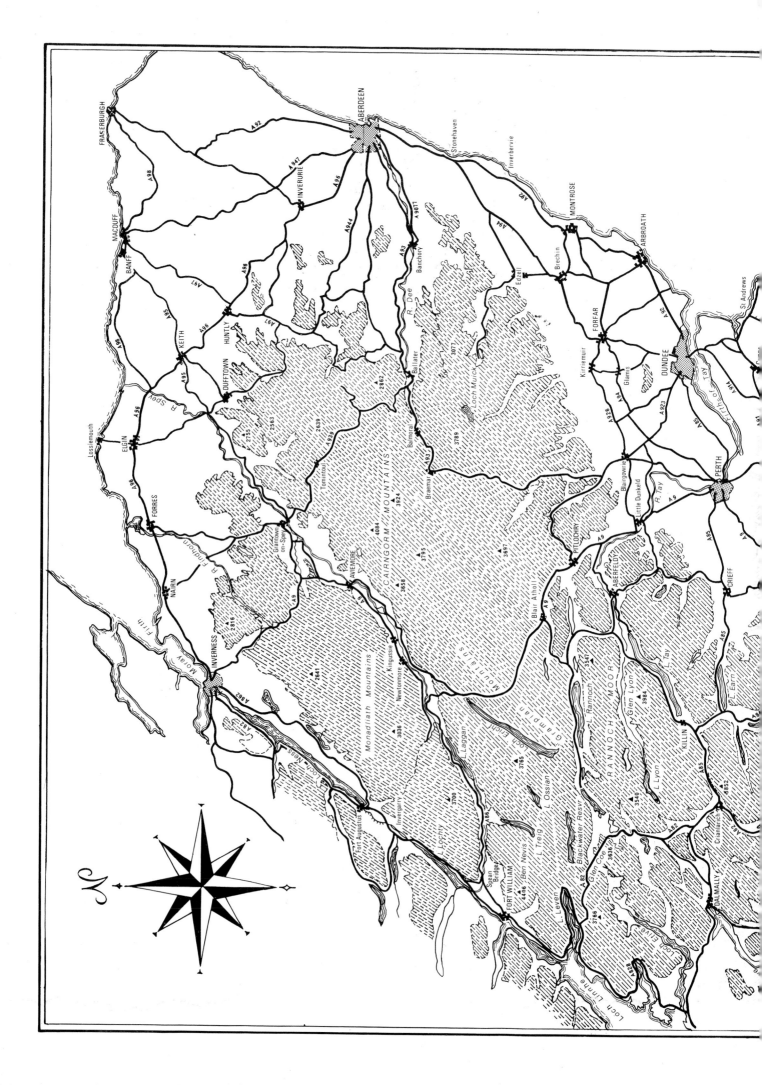